RAMADAN
Bedtime Stories
THIRTY STORIES FOR THIRTY NIGHTS

Copyright

Author: Zainab Mohamed
Title: Ramadan Bedtime Stories
© 2022, Zainab Mohamed

All rights reserved.

No part of this publication may be reproduced, stored in a retrieval system, stored in a database and / or published in any form or by any means, electronic, mechanical, photocopying, recording or otherwise, without the prior written permission of the publisher.

TABLE OF CONTENTS :

INTRODUCTION 07
Chapter 01 : Leila's First Ramadan 10
Chapter 02 : The Story of Prophet Adam (AS) 15
Chapter 03 : Honesty 17
Chapter 04 : The Story of Prophet Nuh (AS) 20
Chapter 05 : Sympathy 22
Chapter 06 : The Story of Prophet Ibrahim (AS) 26
Chapter 07 : Honoring Parents 29
Chapter 08 : The Story of Prophet Yusuf (AS) 32
Chapter 09 : Patience 35
Chapter 10 : Hajar and the Well of Zamzam 39
Chapter 11 : Seeking Permission 41
Chapter 12 : The Story of Prophet Yunus (AS) 45
Chapter 13 : Humility 47
Chapter 14 : A Good Word 51
Chapter 15 : The Story of Prophet Sulayman (AS) 54
Chapter 16 : Ashab Al-Kahf 57
Chapter 17 : The Story of Prophet Isa (AS) 60
Chapter 18 : Respect for the Elderly 62
Chapter 19 : Cooperation 66
Chapter 20 : Laylat Al-Qadr 69
Chapter 21 : Prophet Muhammad ﷺ (Part One) 72
Chapter 22 : Prophet Muhammad ﷺ (Part Two) 75

TABLE OF CONTENTS :

Chapter 23 : Kindness to People 78
Chapter 24 : Loving Your Family 81
Chapter 25 : Don't Make Fun of People 84
Chapter 26 : Saying in Sha' Allah 87
Chapter 27 : Justice Between People 90
Chapter 28 : Learn to Share 94
Chapter 29 : Being Neighborly 97
Chapter 30 : The Blessed Eid 99
CONCLUSION 102

بسم الله الرحمن الرحيم

— IN THE NAME OF ALLAH —

INTRODUCTION

Since the beginning of times, stories have been passed down from generation to generation in order to preserve history and teach humankind important lessons. Stories bring these lessons to life and make them easy for children to absorb. Religion is one of the most difficult concepts to teach to young children, but stories help make this task simple and enjoyable.

Ramadan is a special time of the year when we refresh our beliefs and improve our practice of Islam. This is also a time when children become aware of changes in daily routines as we alter our schedules to accommodate new mealtimes and extra acts of worship. Including our children in Islamic activities throughout the month helps introduce them to fasting and also builds feelings of attachment to Islam and the local Muslim community as they give charity, recite the Quran, and attend the mosque for prayers.

This book has been written with the intention of assisting parents and other caretakers as they guide their children through the blessed month of Ramadan. There are thirty stories in total, with each one presenting a unique and beautiful aspect of Islamic teachings that is important for the development of a young child's Muslim identity. The stories are simple to understand and present scenarios that children can easily relate to.

For maximum benefit, we would advise you to first read each story on your own before reading it to the children in your care, choosing one story for each of the thirty days of Ramadan.

The stories contain numerous opportunities for reflection, both at bedtime and during the day. Although these are "bedtime" stories, teachers, too, may also wish to read these stories out loud to their students in Islamic schools.

Some of the stories portray key incidents from the lives of Allah's prophets and mention the miracles they performed. These stories educate readers about the hardships that the prophets faced in various situations and show how they remained steadfast in their faith in Allah SWT. Several stories focus on the greatness of Prophet Muhammad ﷺ and depict the kindness that he showed to the unbelievers despite their unkind ways, while a number of stories also introduce readers to the Prophet's faithful Companions (may Allah be pleased with them all), who remain shining beacons of righteousness for us to learn from until this day. The greatest lessons in this book come from such stories, as they help children become familiar with the impeccable morals of our beloved Prophet ﷺ and those who followed in his footsteps. Many of this book's stories also take place in modern-day fictional settings in which the characters model the good behaviors we wish for our children to emulate.

The book has been carefully written to make sure that children can relate to the stories easily. In addition, the stories will help stimulate children's curiosity and encourage them to ask questions that will help them understand each story's intended message more clearly. While these messages will naturally sometimes be better understood by children over the age of five (and sometimes even a bit older than that), even younger children will be able to visualize and enjoy the stories.

Prepare yourself, however, because you may soon find that your children's questions lead you to start sharing valuable long-forgotten memories, lessons, and experiences from your own childhood!

Enjoy these precious moments with your children as they begin a fantastic journey on the path of Islamic education and enlightenment through this vivid assortment of stories for each day of Ramadan. It won't be long, in sha' Allah, before your little ones become more aware of the key Islamic values introduced in this book, which uses the ancient art of storytelling to build engagement and interest in a simple yet effective manner!

CHAPTER One

LEILA'S FIRST RAMADAN

"Mama, can you come play dolls with me?" asked six-year-old Leila.

"Not now, sweetie. I'm a little busy at the moment," her mother replied, rushing around and cleaning up like she usually did when they were having special guests over.

Leila went to her brother's room next. She knocked on his door and opened it to find him busy with his laptop.

"Ahmed? Will you come play with me?"

"Sorry, little one, but I'm trying to get my assignments done as fast as I can. Once Ramadan starts, I want to be focused on my worship," said Ahmed, his gaze going back to his laptop.

Leila dragged herself back to her room, sad and confused. No one would play with her, and she didn't even know what was going on. Why was everyone so busy cleaning and working? What was Ramadan, and why did everything need to be finished before it began?

Dinnertime came around, and there was no sign of Leila. Her mother called out her name a few times and then went to look for her. Leila was on her bed, arms folded with a very grumpy look on her face.

"No one will play with me or tell me what Ramadan is!" she said sadly.

"Oh, sweetie!" Leila's mother sat down and took her into her lap. "You know how Muslims do certain things because Allah blesses us for doing them?"

"Sure! Like when we offer salat and do kind things to get rewards in Jannah!" Leila exclaimed.

"Yes, exactly like that. So, during the month of Ramadan, we fast all day from Fajr to Maghrib. Do you know what fasting means?"

"Nope!" said Leila, her tiny nose quivering with excitement.

"Fasting means that we stop doing certain things. We stop eating and drinking and abstain from bad deeds that Allah may not like."

"You mean we can't eat at all?" Leila asked, her eyes round with surprise.

"We can eat before Fajr prayer, and this meal is called the suhur. Then when we hear the Maghrib adhan, we break our fasts and eat a meal called the iftar. But we don't eat anything at all between these two meals."

"But, why?" Leila asked, confused. "We have food at home, don't we?"

"Yes, of course we do, my dear," said Leila's mother with a gentle laugh. "We have plenty of food, al-hamdu-lillah. But when we don't eat for a period of time, this helps us understand what it is like for people who do not have as much as we have. Ramadan teaches us to be kind to the poor and others who may be less fortunate!"

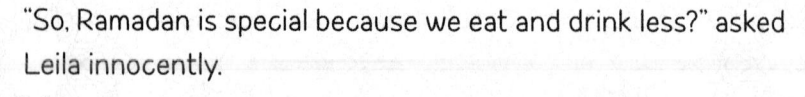

"So, Ramadan is special because we eat and drink less?" asked Leila innocently.

"That's not all there is to it, my dear," said Leila's father as he entered the room. "You see, Ramadan is like a teacher. We learn so many great things from this blessed month. We give more charity. We try to be patient with each other, and we also try to offer extra prayers. The more good deeds and acts of kindness we do each day, the more Allah rewards us."

"So, suhur happens when I am asleep, but that's not fair! Can I wake up for suhur, too?" Leila asked, jumping around in excitement.

"Sure you can, my love," said Leila's father, kissing her on the head. They had dinner, and Leila went to sleep, still giddy with excitement.

Several hours later, when it was still dark outside, Leila's mother woke her up. "Leila, wake up sweetie-pie. It's time for the suhur!"

Leila was up the minute she heard her mother's voice. She'd been so excited that she had barely slept all night.

Leila sat at the table with everyone else. Even though she wasn't very hungry, her mother encouraged her to have some dates and a small bowl of cereal followed by a glass of water so that she would stay hydrated throughout the day and have enough energy to fast.

Afterward, she prayed the Fajr prayer with her family and then went back to sleep.

When Leila woke up again later in the morning, she was surprisingly hungry! She went into the kitchen and found her brother.

"Ahmed, I'm hungry." Leila hid her face behind her hands as her tummy growled.

Ahmed laughed as he gently moved Leila's hands so that he could see her eyes. "It's all right, little one! You can fast the whole day when you get as big as me. Right now, eat what you want."

Leila followed her mother around the whole day long, trying to help in any way she could. Later in the evening, she put some of her best toys into a big bag and went looking for her father. "Can we go give my toys to the children who don't have any?" she asked. "I can't fast, but I can do this good deed, can't I?" Her father hugged her and took her to a shelter, where she gave her toys away to the children who lived there.

At iftar time, everyone broke his or her fast by eating a date. "Baba, why is everyone eating dates?"

"It's a sunnah. You know what a sunnah is, right?"

"Yes! It is doing what Prophet Muhammad, peace be upon him, used to do, and Allah blesses us for these deeds!" Leila said with a wide smile.

"Exactly!" said Leila's father, getting up from the table. "Come on, it's time for Maghrib prayer."

At night, Leila lay down in bed next to her mother, tired and happy. "Mama, that was the best day ever! Can we do Ramadan every day?"

"We still have the whole month left," Leila's mother said with a laugh. "But the reason we do so many good deeds in Ramadan is so that we can get used to doing good deeds all throughout the year. This is why we pray more, read more Quran, and give more in charity. We also try to be kinder and more patient with people. Allah loves those who try to follow in the footsteps of Prophet Muhammad, may the peace and blessings of Allah be upon him."

CHAPTER Two

THE STORY OF PROPHET ADAM (AS)

The story of Adam (AS) is the story of the beginning of humankind.

Allah SWT created the first man, Adam (AS), from clay. After creating Adam (AS) from clay, Allah SWT gave him life and honored him. He honored Adam (AS) by asking the angels to prostrate before him. It was at this point that Iblis rebelled and refused to obey Allah SWT, and he did not prostate before Adam (AS).

Adam (AS) was the first person to ever say Salam! Salam is a greeting of peace that is now said by Muslims all over the world, no matter where they live and which language they speak. Adam (AS) said, "As-salamu alaykum" [Peace be upon you] to a gathering of angels, and they replied, "Wa-alaykum as-salamu wa-rahmatu Allahi wa-barakatuhu" [And peace be upon you as well, along with the mercy and blessings of Allah]. This united all Muslims forever!

Allah SWT created Hawwa as a companion for Adam (AS), and they lived together in Paradise. In Paradise, they had all the blessings one could imagine. Allah SWT had forbidden them both from ever eating any fruit from a specific tree there, but Iblis was determined to make sure he distracted Adam (AS) and Hawwa from following the way of Allah. Iblis succeeded at distracting them, and they went to the tree and tasted the forbidden fruit.

After this, Allah SWT banished Adam (AS) and Hawwa from Paradise. Devastated, they begged Allah SWT for His forgiveness, and He forgave them.

Adam (AS) was the first human being on Earth, and he was the first in a long line of prophets as well. Adam (AS) preached the Word of Allah SWT throughout his life.

The lesson we learn from Adam's story is that we should seek forgiveness from Allah SWT whenever we make mistakes. He is Most Gracious and Most Merciful!

CHAPTER
Three

HONESTY

It was bright and early on a crisp winter day. Faris looked out from his window to see fresh snow sparkling in the sun. "Faris, have you brushed your teeth?" his mother called out. "Come down quickly, or your bus will leave you behind!"

"Coming, Mom!" Faris yelled back in response.

After a mug of milk and a soft-boiled egg, Faris packed up his bag and ran out into the cold wind before running back inside. He had forgotten his scarf—again! He stepped into the warm bus and sat down next to his best friend, Musa. The two boys chattered about the new video game they were playing. When Faris was just about to get off the bus, a big boy named Haris stuck his foot out.

Faris tripped and landed on the curbside, grazing his elbow. Faris was very upset. Musa quickly came and helped Faris up. He could see that he was very angry. Faris said, "He always does that! What have I ever done to him?"

Musa replied, "I know man, but let it go. We're getting late for class." Faris stomped his feet all the way to the classroom.

All through class, Faris's elbow ached from the fall. He still felt angry about what had happened and would not play tic-tac-toe with Musa and did not even laugh at his jokes. He was just very, very angry!

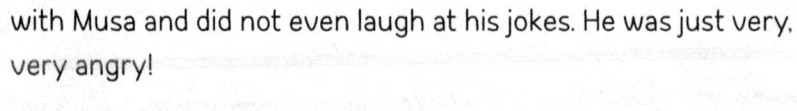

At recess, Faris and his friends were playing soccer, and the big boys were sitting on the bleachers jeering at the younger boys playing in the field. Once recess was over, they headed back inside. Faris saw that big boy Haris who kept tripping him in the bus—and Faris decided to retaliate. He stuck his foot out, and the boy fell. But he fell really hard—much harder than Faris expected. He slipped on a patch of ice and hit his head. His forehead began to bleed.

Ms. Qasim, the class teacher, quickly rushed to Haris's side. She helped the boy up and took him to the school nurse's office.

Faris and Musa went back to their classroom. Faris began to feel ill. He had not meant to hurt Haris so badly, and he did not know what to do. When Ms. Qasim came back, she was not smiling. She turned to the class and said solemnly, "Haris is all right, but he did get hurt really badly. Can someone please tell me what happened?"

Faris was afraid. His hands were shaking, and he felt very uncomfortable. Musa was looking at Faris quietly. But Faris did not say anything. The bell rang, signaling it was time to go home.

That evening, Faris was unusually quiet at the dinner table. His mother asked, "Faris, are you feeling okay?"

"Yes, Mom," he replied. "I just don't feel like eating. Can I please leave the table?"

"Sure!" said Faris's mother, still very concerned. Faris got into bed, but he felt terrible. He felt badly for tripping Haris, and he felt terrible for not telling his teacher the truth. And now, he just could not sleep.

Faris's father knocked on the door and came inside the room. He sat on Faris's bed and asked, "What's the matter, son?" Faris got up, hugged his father, and began to sob. Once his tears subsided, he told his father everything that had happened.

"Son, when we hide the truth, it makes us feel uncomfortable. You should go to your teacher tomorrow and tell her the truth about what happened. She will understand, and you will feel better. Remember that our Prophet, may the peace and blessings of Allah be upon him, was very particular about being honest and never telling lies."

The next day, Faris went to his teacher and told her the truth. She was very pleased with his honesty. Then Faris went to Haris and apologized. "Haris, I am very sorry for what I did," said Faris. "I should have never tripped you. It was wrong of me, and I hope you are feeling better now."

Haris replied, "I am the one who should be sorry for tripping you so many times, Faris. I will tell Ms. Qasim that I started this."

Faris replied, "Well, let's be friends now and not hurt each other!"

Allah SWT loves those who are honest. Because Faris was honest, he ended up with a great new friend! He also found out that honesty is very rewarding and puts the heart at ease.

CHAPTER Four

THE STORY OF PROPHET NUH (AS)

Prophet Nuh (AS) was one of the many glorious prophets of Allah SWT. He was sent to a land where the people did not believe in One God. They used to make statues with their own hands and then worship them as idols. Nuh (AS) spent many years preaching to his people about Allah SWT and how He was the only one worthy of worship, but most people refused to believe. Instead, they made fun of Nuh (AS) and ridiculed him, while only a few among the poor and humble believed him and began to follow his teachings. Even after many years of hard work, only a few people began to follow him on the path of righteousness.

Nuh (AS) continuously prayed to Allah SWT for help. Eventually, Allah SWT commanded Nuh (AS) to build a boat, which he did with the blessed guidance of Allah. The disbelievers thought this was very amusing because they were on dry land, and there was no water nearby at all!

But Nuh (AS) knew that huge amounts of water would soon pour down from the sky to punish those who disbelieved in the Oneness of Allah SWT, so he ignored what the disbelievers were saying and continued working hard to finish building the huge boat.

When the boat was ready, Allah SWT told Nuh (AS) to bring several different pairs of various animals with him on the boat, along with all of the people who believed in Allah SWT. When they were ready, the animals all entered the boat one after the other.

Once they were all safely in the boat, it slowly started to rain. Angry black clouds came rolling in as the drizzle turned into storms and heavy rains. The wind blew from all directions, and the sky became dark. There was water as far as the eye could see—huge waves of it! As it rained from the heavens, the ground also cracked open, and water came out from below. The water rose higher and higher until the trees and mountains drowned under the flood of water. All of the people who had not listened to Nuh's message and remained on land drowned as well.

Although the boat floated safely, the believers inside of it were very scared. There was lightning, thunder, and strong winds as water crashed down from all sides. But Nuh (AS) remained steadfast in his faith and prayed to Allah SWT to help them through this trial.

When the flood had carried out its purpose, Allah SWT made the sky hold back its rain as the ground opened up and swallowed back its water. The rain stopped, and the clouds cleared. The mountains were visible again, and the boat stopped on the peak of a mountain. The animals slowly climbed out, and the people followed, grateful to be alive, and thankful to Allah SWT for His mercy.

CHAPTER
Five

SYMPATHY

Everyone was sitting around the dinner table when Ehsan struck up a conversation.

"There's a new kid in my class named Shoaib."

"Really?" asked Ehsan's mother, surprised. "In the middle of the school year?"

Ehsan shrugged. "Our teacher said that he moved here with his family from another city."

"Well, did he tell you why?" asked Ehsan's father.

"Not really! He's a weird kid though," Ehsan mumbled.

"Why would you say that—especially about someone whom you just met?" Mama scolded him.

"If you were there in the classroom, you would be saying the same thing!" Ehsan replied.

"Okay, then, tell us what is so weird about your new classmate," said Baba, trying to conceal his curiosity.

Ehsan thought for a moment and said, "First of all, he can't read anything properly. He is also messy and doesn't play with any of the other kids. Some kids said he was dumb."

While Baba was thinking about a suitable response, Mama said, "Sometimes people are struggling with certain things, and they just need another person to listen and help them with their problems. Do you think it is ever okay to be mean to someone who struggling to learn and communicate?"

She looked around the table before continuing. "What if you were in his shoes?" she asked Ehsan pointedly. "How would you feel if people were saying the same things about you?"

Ehsan lowered his eyes in shame and said, "I apologize for what I said. Maybe I can try to be friends with him if he is okay with that."

"I think that's a wonderful idea!" said Baba enthusiastically. "When you sympathize with people and try to understand them, you make them feel more at ease. Shoaib is new to your class, so you should do your best to make him feel welcome."

The next day at school, Ehsan waited for lunchtime before approaching Shoaib. "As-salamu alaykum!" he told him. "My name is Ehsan."

Shoaib gazed at him warily and did not reply.

"Don't worry, I don't want to bother you or anything. I just wanted to talk to you. Maybe we can be friends."

Again, silence.

Ehsan was about to give up and walk away when Shoaib reluctantly opened his mouth to speak. "Why do you want to be my friend?" he asked.

"Oh! Because you're new here, and I thought maybe you could use a friend," said Ehsan with a smile.

"I know some kids think that I am weird and dumb. They do not want to play with me or even talk to me."

Ehsan felt a little guilty. "I'm sure they will change their minds once they get to know you," he said.

Shoaib had a sad look on his face. "I'm not dumb, by the way. I have dyslexia."

"What is that?" Ehsan asked, confused.

"It's a learning disability. I have trouble recognizing letters, so it is a big challenge for me to read and write. This sometimes makes it difficult to understand what the teacher is talking about."

"I am so sorry you have to go through that every day," said Ehsan sincerely.

Shoaib shrugged. "I am used to it. We move a lot because of my father's job. So, it was difficult for me to get diagnosed. We finally figured it out a few months ago, and now I am getting the help I need to overcome this challenge."

"Maybe we could study together sometimes, and I could help you as well," Ehsan offered.

Shoaib smiled. "I would like that very much," he said, his eyes gleaming with happiness.

That evening, Ehsan went home and told his mother what had happened at lunchtime. "Mama, our deen teaches us to be kind to people. We should always try to sympathize with them and not judge them or make fun of them. I feel really badly because of my behavior. I am sorry!"

"The important thing is that you remembered to be kind in the end," said Mama with a tearful smile. "As Muslims, it is never too late for us to work on our flaws and shortcomings—and it is a blessing from Allah when we know how to empathize with others and show understanding for their difficulties, because this is what allows us to help and support them. I am so proud of you for doing the right thing."

Ehsan nodded and vowed to do better.

CHAPTER Six

THE STORY OF PROPHET IBRAHIM (AS)

Prophet Ibrahim (AS) was one of the most beloved prophets of Allah SWT. When he was a little boy, everyone around him worshiped idols. Ibrahim (AS) was a very smart and clever little boy. He thought it was very strange that the people built the idols with their own hands and then worshiped them as gods. If these so-called "gods" needed humans to create them, did that mean that humans were more powerful than Allah? It was all very strange and confusing.

One day, Ibrahim (AS) decided that he would try to figure out who Allah was by himself. He saw the twinkling stars in the night-sky and was sure they must be Allah. But they disappeared with the sunrise, so they certainly could not be Allah.

Then when night fell again and Ibrahim (AS) saw the moon, he thought that the moon was so beautiful that it surely must be Allah. But when morning came, the moon was gone just like the stars. He realized that something that left when morning came could certainly not be Allah. With that, he decided that the sun must be Allah, but the sun went away at night, so it too could not be Allah!

Ibrahim (AS) came to the conclusion that Allah could not be seen; one just had to believe. Allah SWT was the One who had created the stars, the moon, and the sun. If these things created by Allah were so magnificent, then what about the Creator of these things? Surely, Allah was the most magnificent of all!

One day, when all of the men were elsewhere, Ibrahim (AS) took an axe and destroyed all of the idols, except for the biggest one. Then he placed the axe in its hands.

The people were shocked when they returned. They asked Ibrahim (AS) what had happened. He told them to ask the idol with the axe in its hands.

Ibrahim's father was furious. "You know very well that it cannot speak!" he told Ibrahim (AS).

Ibrahim (AS) asked him, "If it cannot speak or do anything for itself, why do you worship it?"

The people were very angry and decided that Ibrahim (AS) must be punished. So, they built a very large blazing fire and threw Ibrahim (AS) into the fire!

Ibrahim (AS) knew that Allah SWT was with him, so he remained steadfast as this happened.

Allah SWT protects those who show faith in Him—and, lo and behold, the fire was not hot! Allah SWT had ordered the fire to cool down for Ibrahim (AS). He stayed in the fire for many days until it burned out completely and then walked out to the shock of the disbelievers.

After that, many people started following the teachings of Ibrahim (AS) and understood that they must abandon the worship of idols and worship Allah SWT instead.

Ibrahim (AS) left that land and went to different places to preach the Oneness and Truth of Allah SWT. Later, Allah SWT blessed Ibrahim (AS) with a son named Ismail (AS). He, too, was a prophet of Allah SWT, and they spent their lives worshiping Allah SWT.

CHAPTER *Seven*

HONORING PARENTS

It was Parents' Day at school, and the celebration was exciting and full of fun. Children and teachers were scurrying around, making sure that all of the students who were performing in the play were ready to showcase their acting talents. Many beautiful projects were also on display throughout the classrooms and hallways.

Ms. Yasmin, the arts teacher, was checking every detail of the event. Her hands were endlessly busy, fixing a girl's ponytail, reminding another to tuck in her blouse, and adjusting some of the displays to maximize their visual appeal.

She was rushing toward the stage when she noticed little Yasir sitting off to the side with his head hanging low, almost hiding behind the props set in front of him. She was about to pass by, but something made her stop. It was the little boy's tears dripping down his cheeks.

Heart aching, she kneeled down next to him and said, "What happened, sweetheart? Why are you sitting here alone?"

Stumbling over his words, Yasir said, "Salam, Ms. Yasmin," and then quickly sat up straight and wiped the tears from his face.

"Wa-alaykum as-salam! Are you doing okay, little munchkin?" asked Ms. Yasmin.

"I'm fine," he mumbled back.

"Is it the play? If you're nervous about your lines, I could help you review them," she offered.

"No, I am sure I remember all of my lines," he replied.

"Okay! Well, I am just going to help prepare the lights and costumes in the back room. Are your parents here yet?"

It was like a dam had burst open. Yasir started crying and couldn't stop.

Ms. Yasmin hugged him tightly until he finally found the strength to speak. "My parents... died a long time ago... in a car accident... when I was still little," he said slowly.

Ms. Yasmin could feel her eyes getting moist. She cleared her throat and said, "Oh, sweetie! I am so sorry for your loss. Inna li-llahi wa-inna ilayhi rajioun. May Allah bless your parents with the highest ranks of Jannah. Amin. I wish you had told me! There was no need for you to participate in today's activities if you did not want to. It makes me sad that you are feeling so hurt."

"No, I'm fine," said Yasir bravely. "I'm actually okay. It happened a long time ago, and that's not what's making me sad."

"Okay then, what is it?" Ms. Yasmin held Yasir's hand and squeezed it.

"You said earlier that Parents' Day is about making our parents proud. And I can't do that because they are not here." His chin wobbled a bit.

"Oh, honey, no. That's not true at all. There are so many ways to honor your parents and make them proud even if they are no longer alive!"

"There are?" Yasir felt a little ray of hope stir inside of him.

"Yes, of course! You can honor your parents by doing all of the good things they taught you! That would make them very proud of you. Did you know that your parents get rewarded each time you do something good that they taught you? Imagine all of the rewards they will earn every time you pray or are kind to someone or follow the sunnah. Pray to Allah for His mercy and blessings upon them, and they will be surprised and happy to see all of the rewards they have earned on the final Day of Judgement!"

"That makes me so happy!" Yasir beamed. "Jazaki Allah khayr, Ms. Yasmin." He hugged her tightly.

She hugged him back and thanked Allah SWT for giving her a student like him.

CHAPTER
Eight

THE STORY OF PROPHET YUSUF (AS)

Yusuf (AS) was a prophet of Allah SWT and one of the most beautiful men ever created.

He descended from a chain of prophets that started with Ibrahim (AS) (his great-grandfather) and continued with Ishaq (AS) (his grandfather), then Yaqub (AS) (his father), and finally him. He was strong, handsome, and a righteous person within his household. He had eleven brothers, one of whom may have been named Binyamin. His father loved all of his children; however, Yusuf (AS) and Binyamin had a little extra space inside of his heart that distinguished them from the rest.

Once, when Yusuf (AS) was a young boy, he had a dream that the sun, the moon, and eleven stars were bowing down to him. He quickly approached his father and told him about the dream. Yaqub (AS) understood from his description of the dream that Yusuf (AS) would one day become a prophet—but he warned him not to tell his brothers as they would be very jealous of him.

Yusuf's brothers were indeed jealous of him even though they didn't know about the dream. So, one day they decided to throw Yusuf (AS) into a well. They went to their father and asked if Yusuf (AS) could go play with them. Yaqub (AS) wanted to say no because he was worried about wolves in the area that hunted the sheep, but his sons begged him until he couldn't say no.

The brothers all left together, but once they were far away, they grabbed Yusuf (AS) and threw him into the well. They tore off his shirt and slaughtered a sheep and rubbed all of the blood on the shirt. Then they went to their father crying and said that a wolf had eaten their brother while they were playing, showing him Yusuf's bloody shirt as proof.

Yaqub (AS) became very sad; however, he knew that his son Yusuf (AS) was alive, and that his other sons were lying. He prayed to Allah SWT to help Yusuf (AS) wherever he was and not let him fall into despair or lose hope in the blessings of Allah SWT.

Yusuf (AS) was all alone and scared in the well. By Allah's will, however, a caravan of merchants passing by on its way to Egypt soon stopped for water. The merchants found Yusuf (AS) in the well and decided to take him with them as a slave. Later, a very rich man purchased Yusuf (AS) and took him to his palace, where he treated him well.

Yusuf (AS) grew up to be the most handsome man anyone had ever seen. The lady of the house wanted him to commit a sin—a big sin that would make Allah SWT very displeased. When Yusuf (AS) refused, the woman became very angry. She decided to punish Yusuf (AS) and banished him to a prison cell. Yusuf (AS) stayed in jail for many years and told people about Allah SWT. He also learned to read and interpret people's dreams.

One day, the king needed to know the meaning of a dream, and Yusuf (AS) was able to help him. He told the king that the dream meant that they would have an abundance of food for seven years followed by seven years of famine, so they should try to store as much grain as possible whenever supplies were plentiful.

The king found this news very astonishing. He took Yusuf (AS) out of jail and put him in charge of storing food.

Years later, when Yusuf (AS) was distributing food to the needy, his brothers also showed up asking for food. Yusuf (AS) tricked Binyamin into staying behind and told him who he was, which made Binyamin very happy. The rest of Yusuf's brothers went back to their father, who became very sad when they returned without Binyamin. He wept so profusely when he found out that Binyamin was also missing that he went blind and could no longer see.

The brothers went back to Yusuf (AS) and begged him to return their brother to them. He finally told them who he was, and they were shocked and ashamed. They begged him for forgiveness, and he forgave them.

Yaqub (AS) traveled to Egypt with the rest of his family, and they were all very happy to see Yusuf (AS) alive and safe. They bowed down to him, just like what he had seen in his dream so many years before. Yusuf's miraculous dream had finally come true.

CHAPTER
Nine

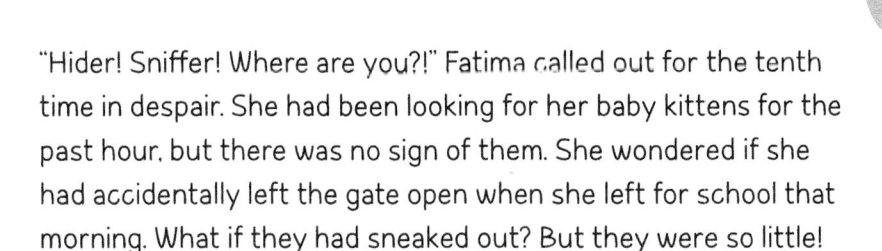

PATIENCE

"Hider! Sniffer! Where are you?!" Fatima called out for the tenth time in despair. She had been looking for her baby kittens for the past hour, but there was no sign of them. She wondered if she had accidentally left the gate open when she left for school that morning. What if they had sneaked out? But they were so little!

"What if someone took them? Or, Allah forbid, a car ran over them?" she murmured to herself looking around frantically. "No, no, no," she thought, shaking her head. She would not allow the Shaytan to put thoughts of despair into her head. Surely, Allah the Most Merciful, the Protector, would look after her tiny, innocent pets.

But as the day wore on, Fatima grew more and more sad. She went out to call her kittens again, and there were no answering meows. She tried again just as the sun was setting, but there was no sound of the tiny bells that tinkled around their necks when they would race toward her, eager to play. Fatima wiped her eyes and went back inside with a heavy heart.

At night, she hid her face in her pillow and wept. She missed the sound of her little kitties purring in their basket by her bed. Thinking about her little fur babies and what they might be going through made her cry even harder.. Fatima's mother came and brushed back her hair and gave her a kiss on the forehead. When Fatima eventually calmed down, her mother said, "It's okay to cry and be sad when we miss someone we love."

"But Mama, do you think that Allah would prefer that I be patient instead?" Fatima asked hesitantly.

"You can be both sad and patient at the same time," her mother replied.

"Really?" Fatima was surprised. "How?" she asked.

"Do you remember the story of Prophet Yusuf, alayhi as-salam?"

Fatima said, "Some of it. Can you tell please tell it to me again?"

"Well, my dear, Yusuf's brothers were jealous of him because their father, Prophet Yaqub, alayhi as-salam, loved him the most. So, they threw him in a well to die and told their father that a wolf had eaten him. He didn't believe them, and he was right not to. Do you know how many years later they were reunited with each other?"

Fatima, who was listening with wide-eyed attention, shook her head.

"Forty years! And, do you think that his father never cried for him at all during that long period of time? No, in fact, he did cry. He cried so much that he eventually lost his eyesight and became blind. But he still couldn't stop crying for the son that he missed with all his heart. But he also prayed to Allah. His patience was so great and long-lasting that Allah called his patience sabrun jameel, which means 'beautiful patience.' So, we can definitely be patient and sad at the same time. We can even cry so long as we have faith in Allah. So, be certain that Allah will protect our little kittens even if you miss them badly."

"I love that story. Thank you, Mama! The funny feeling in my tummy hurts less now."

"Al-hamdu-lillah!" said Mama and left Fatima with her sweet thoughts to sleep.

Fatima woke up the next morning and suddenly felt sad again, but then she remembered the story Mama had told her and took a deep breath. She was determined to find her precious kittens today!

Allah helps those who help themselves, she told herself. After I come back from school, I'll make posters with their faces and display them all around the neighborhood. Surely someone will have seen them, in sha' Allah.

After breakfast, she was walking toward her front gate when the bell rang. She wondered who it could be so early in the day. She opened the gate and saw a woman standing outside.

"Hello!" She smiled politely and waited for the woman to speak.

"Hello, sweetie. My name is Mary. Do you by any chance happen to be missing two adorable little kittens?" said the woman.

Fatima's eyes nearly popped out of her head as she screeched, "Yes, yes, yes! Have you seen them?"

"Oh boy, have I seen those little troublemakers. They wandered over to my yard yesterday and climbed a tree. Poor things got stuck because they were too afraid to come down. I eventually had to call the fire department, and they rescued the kittens. By the time it was all done with, it was pretty late at night, so I just settled them at my place with my cats. I checked their collars this morning and saw your address written on them." The kind woman laughed as she turned around and started walking back to her car.

As soon as she opened the door, out streaked two furballs who were falling all over themselves to reach Fatima as they meowed and twirled around her legs. She fell to the floor sobbing as she hugged them and thanked the kind woman again and again. Then she looked up at the sky and thanked Allah for answering her prayers.

"Al-hamdu-lillah ya Rabb!"

CHAPTER Ten

HAJAR AND THE WELL OF ZAMZAM

Prophet Ibrahim (AS) was one of the most beloved prophets of Allah SWT. He spent his life in the service of Allah SWT and worked hard to spread Allah's message to the people. He was blessed with a son named Ismail (AS). The love he had for his son was great, but the love he had for Allah SWT was even greater.

One day, Allah SWT ordered Ibrahim (AS) to travel to a faraway place with his wife Hajar and their son Ismail (AS), who was still a baby at the time. They eventually reached a barren valley. There was no food, water, or shelter anywhere in the valley. Allah SWT told Ibrahim (AS) to leave his family there and go away. Hajar asked him if he was leaving because Allah had ordered him to do so. When the answer was yes, she was content with this. Despite the great hardship of being left without any food, water, or shelter, she had faith that Allah would not leave them helpless and alone.

After a while, baby Ismail (AS) got thirsty and started crying. Hajar started looking around for water, but there was none to be found. She climbed to the top of a hilly peak known as Mount Safa and looked for someone to help her, but saw no one. She then ran to the top of another mountain called Marwah. Again, she saw nothing.

Hajar ran back and forth between the two mountains seven times looking for water for her son, but to no avail. It is because of Hajar's great effort and unwavering faith in Allah that we perform the same act during the pilgrimages of Hajj and Umrah.

After the seventh time, Hajar saw an angel standing next to baby Ismail (AS). Her heart swelled with hope that Allah SWT had answered her prayers. The angel struck the ground next to them, and a spring of water came gushing out.

This was the well that is known to Muslims as Zamzam. Many centuries later, we still drink from the abundant waters of Zamzam until this very day. This blessing from Allah SWT is very special and contains many healing properties. As people began to hear about the water, Hajar's dwelling place slowly began to grow as a community in the vast desert. This is the same land known to us as Makkah.

When Ismail (AS) grew up, Ibrahim (AS) told him that it was time for them to build the House of Allah.

So, Ismail (AS) gathered the stones while Ibrahim (AS) set them in their place. When the walls became too high, Ismail (AS) brought a stone for his father to stand upon so that he could continue working. They continued to build this House of Allah until it was finished. The Kaabah has since been the center of worship for all Muslims around the world during prayers and the pilgrimages of Hajj and Umrah.

CHAPTER Eleven

SEEKING PERMISSION

Amina loved her mother's jewelry and other pretty things. She would watch as her mother carefully put the lovely trinkets away after wearing them and knew that they were very precious to her. Some were gifts from Dad, and some were things that Granny had given her when she was a little girl.

Mommy had told Amina that it was okay to look at her things when she was there, but not to touch them, because some of the items were very valuable and were so tiny that they could easily get lost.

One afternoon, Mommy went out to visit Aunty Sara, who was unwell. Before leaving, Mommy said, "Amina, dearest, please play safely at home, and don't touch anything that can harm you. Also, please ask for permission if you need anything from Aunty Maryam. She will be taking care of you and the house today." With that, she gave Amina a kiss and left.

Amina played with her dolls, and then with her tablet, for a long time, but then she got bored. She asked Aunty Maryam if she could go to the park to play, but she replied, "Sweetie, I am feeling tired today. I can't take you while I have this awful headache, and you can't go alone—so please be a good girl and play inside." But Amina was not feeling very happy about being told no.

She made a sulky face and went to her room. Suddenly, she remembered something! Mommy's things! Amina loved playing dress-up and had a box of Mommy's old clothes to herself that she could use to pretend she was Mommy. Amina's mother had told her to never touch her jewelry. But Amina wanted the pretty blue pin from the jewelry box!

She dragged a chair to the dresser and climbed on top in order to open the box. The lovely blue pin glittered in the light, and Amina picked it up. She fastened the pin to her frock and began pretending she was Mommy. She peered downstairs and saw Aunty Maryam resting her aching head. Amina, quiet as a mouse, left the house to go play in the park.

In the park, she met her friends, Samia and Maimoona. The two girls saw the glittering pin and were very impressed. They asked where she got it from, and Amina happily replied that she had borrowed it from her mother. The three girls began to play with the pin. Soon, they forgot about the pin and began playing tag. They ran around the park, all helter-skelter. Before long, it began to get dark and cold.

Amina rushed back home to a very angry Aunty Maryam. She was scolded for leaving the house without permission. This made Amina very grumpy, and she refused to eat anything. Then she heard the car tires crackle on the gravel. Mommy was home! But her elation soon turned to panic when she suddenly remembered the blue pin! Amina looked everywhere, but she could not find it. She could not even remember where she had left it! She was in big trouble now.

When she saw Mommy, she began to sob. Mommy was very worried and asked, "Amina, what is the matter?" Too frightened to tell Mommy what had happened, Amina sobbed even louder. Finally, she did tell her. When she looked up, Mommy's face was very sad and disappointed. Amina knew that the pin was very special, but she felt helpless and did not know what to do. Daddy heard the story and took a big flashlight with him to the park to look for the pin, hoping he would find it.

Mommy quietly made some dinner for Amina and sat her down at the table. Then she said, "Look Amina, I asked you not to touch the jewelry box. It is not polite to take anyone's belongings, and especially without permission. Always remember that Allah is All Knowing and sees all that we do. This means that Allah sees us even when no else is around. You should never disobey Mommy and Daddy. We have your best interests at heart, and this is why we work so hard guide you—because we want you to learn good values that will help you in life."

Amina felt bad—very, very bad. She quietly finished her dinner and went to bed, where she tossed and turned but could not sleep.

Suddenly, she heard the click of the front door and voices. Then she heard Mommy come to her room and say, "Amina, Daddy found the pin. Look!" And there it was, shining in Mommy's hand. Then Mommy said, "Next time, when you want to try something or borrow something, ask for permission! If I had known that you wanted to try the pin so badly, I would have fastened it to your clothing myself, and you could have played inside the house where it would have been safe."

Amina felt better that the pin had been found, but she was very sorry that she had worried Mommy and caused so much trouble. She promised her mother that she would never take anything that belonged to anyone else without permission, and that she would listen to her elders whenever they tried to guide her.

CHAPTER
Twelve

THE STORY OF PROPHET YUNUS (AS)

Yunus (AS) was a renowned prophet of Allah SWT and the only prophet to whom Allah gave an extraordinary punishment. It was due to this punishment that Allah SWT descended His mercy upon his nation after they accepted Islam.

Yunus (AS) was sent to a nation whose people were in the depths of sin with a message to accept the religion of One God, Allah. However, the people of this nation did not accept his message and remained sinful. Yunus (AS) tried his best to convey the message loud and clear to the people, but they did not accept it. He realized that they would never listen to him, so he decided that he would leave his people and go far away. With that, he set off to find different people who would listen to him and believe in his message, but he did not wait for Allah's permission to leave.

Yunus (AS) went to the seaport and found a ship that was going to a faraway place. He boarded the ship, but it wasn't long before the skies got dark and stormy, and the sea began rock. People threw their belongings off of the ship to make it lighter, but their efforts were in vain. Likewise, the sailors tried to keep the ship on course, but the waves were too strong and powerful.

They decided to throw someone overboard to save the ship and chose Yunus (AS) after drawing lots multiple times.

As difficult as this situation was, Yunus (AS) knew that this was happening for a reason, as Allah SWT was surely very displeased with him for leaving his people and giving up on them without Allah's permission. As soon as he was in the water, a huge fish came and swallowed him up whole without biting him!

It was very dark inside the stomach of the fish, but there was so much space that Prophet Yunus (AS) remained alive. He was very scared, so he prayed to Allah and asked him for forgiveness over and over again. The animals around the fish heard the prayer as well and prayed along with him.

Allah SWT blessed Prophet Yunus (AS) with His forgiveness and saved him from the darkness in the stomach of the big fish. By Allah's will, the fish took Prophet Yunus (AS) to an island and gently spat him out. However, due to staying there in the stomach of the fish for three days and three nights, Prophet Yunus's body was hurt. Nevertheless, Allah SWT had kept him alive.

Yunus (AS) went back to his people thinking that Allah SWT would have punished them for not accepting his teachings, but when he arrived, he found that everyone had accepted Islam and now believed in the Oneness of God! He realized that his people had indeed been punished for their sins while he was away, but Allah SWT had forgiven them due to their repentance just as He had also forgiven Yunus (AS) for leaving his people without Allah's permission.

CHAPTER Thirteen

HUMILITY

Sulaiman trudged up the steps to his house, head hanging low. He banged open the front door and dragged his feet inside.

"As-salamu alaykum," a stern voice said pointedly, hearing no salam when he entered.

"Wa-alaykum as-salam," he mumbled back to his sister as he took off his shoes and plopped down on the couch.

"What's up, squirt?" asked Aminah, plopping down on the couch beside him.

Sulaiman sighed and said nothing.

"Come on, what's the matter?"

"Okay, fine," Sulaiman said morosely. "If you must know, I was at Abdul-Rahman's house playing PlayStation, and it was so much fun!"

"Okay, so what's the problem?" Aminah asked, poking him.

"The problem is that I want a PlayStation, too!"

"Oh!" Aminah nodded her head in understanding.

"All of my friends have one, and I'm the only one who doesn't!"

Sulaiman sulked.

"Okay, but why do you want one?" Aminah asked.

Sulaiman stared at her in puzzlement. "What do you mean? I just told you, I want to play on the PlayStation as well!"

"I understand that. But can't you just play at Abdul-Rahman's house?"

"No, I want my own console!" said Sulaiman, kicking the table with his foot.

"Yeah, but why?" Aminah persisted.

"Because!" Sulaiman blurted out. "I don't want to be the only uncool one who doesn't have a PlayStation!"

"Okay, so do you want a PlayStation so that you can actually play on it, or is it just something you want so that you can show off to your friends?"

Sulaiman didn't reply for some time. His mind churned as he thought about his reasons for wanting a PlayStation. "I guess I want one to play with," he said slowly, "But I also want to show it to my friends. I don't want to feel left out. Also, I kind of want everyone to see that I have cool things, too."

"That makes sense." Aminah nodded her head thoughtfully. "It's hard to feel left out when our friends all have something in common, right?"

Sulaiman nodded his head vigorously.

"I would love for you to have to a PlayStation if that's what makes you happy. But I wouldn't want you to have one just so you can show it off to everyone."

"Does it really matter what the reason is?" Sulaiman was genuinely curious to know. "Either way, I would be using it to play my favorite games."

"It always matters. Intention is key to our every act as Muslims, and this means that we should always be aware of our true intentions whenever we do something, because Allah blesses us when we are humble and practice humility."

"What does it mean to practice humility?"

Aminah thought about it for a minute. "Humility is when we try not to be proud and arrogant. Someone who is humble does not ever show off or act better than other people. We must always be conscious of this, because Allah blesses us so much—way beyond what we actually deserve."

"I don't think I'm better than anyone else, though," Sulaiman said, trying to explain his point of view.

"I know you don't, squirt. But pride is that feeling we get when we want to show off something we have done or acquired—and this is bad even if the thing itself is something good. So, we should peek inside of our hearts to see what our true intentions are. Of course, we should also keep in mind that we are only human and will keep making mistakes. And that's okay—so long as we always try to fix things and make them right. "

"So, does that mean no PlayStation?" Sulaiman asked cheekily.

Aminah laughed. "That means maybe you will have a PlayStation one day in the future, in sha' Allah—but for the right reasons."

"In sha' Allah!" said Sulaiman. "For now, I'll play with Abdul-Rahman's console and help him with his homework whenever I can—you know, just for the sake of doing a good deed."

"He is really bad at math," added Sulaiman, shaking his head.

CHAPTER Fourteen

A GOOD WORD

Dad saw Ahmed coming in and asked, "Did you have a good time? Who won?"

"NO ONE!" came a loud yell just before Ahmed slammed his bedroom door.

This was not like Ahmed. His father looked at Ahmed's mother, who was standing in the kitchen with a surprised expression on her face. Dad said, "Let me see what's the matter with the little champ."

THUD! THUD! THUD! THUD!

Dad found Ahmed inside of his room, hitting a ball on the wall and catching it with a particularly grumpy expression on his face.

"Shall we talk?" asked Dad.

"Dad, I am SO angry! I just want to break something!"

Dad calmly caught the ball and sat down on the edge of Ahmed's bed. "And why is that, bud?" he asked.

"You know Qasim and his friends? Those big boys who live down the street? They came to play cricket with us today," said Ahmed, his words racing out of his mouth. "When I bowled, they kept hitting the ball so far away! They scored a million runs—I don't even know how many. Then when they started to bowl, they bowled us out in less than a second!"

"Son, that's perfectly okay—they are big boys! You guys will get better. If anything, I think that was good practice for you. Why are you upset?" asked Dad.

Ahmed gulped and said, "Dad, Qasim was rude to Ali."

Ali was Ahmed's best friend. They had grown up together as next-door neighbors and were like brothers.

"What did they say?" Dad's tone was serious. He knew that Ali was Ahmed's very best friend, and Ahmed was clearly very upset.

"They made fun of him, Dad. They called him names and joked about his shoes. Ali was so upset that he couldn't even say anything. Then when I tried to say something, he pulled me away and told me not to answer them! Dad, he is so dumb! Why didn't he let me fight back?"

Dad smiled and said, "Ali is indeed a great friend!"

"How is that?" grumbled Ahmed.

"You know what one of the best things about being a good Muslim is? It's being kind. Both your deeds and your words should always be kind. No matter what, you should always say something good. But if you don't have anything nice to say, then it is better to remain quiet."

"What good would that do?" asked Ahmed, a little less angry now.

Dad said, "Our Prophet, may the peace and blessings of Allah be upon him, was the kindest person ever—and he taught us to never to say anything that would hurt others. This way, we keep the friends we have and make new ones. The fact that Ali was so patient and helped you learn something good as well shows that he is a very special boy!"

"Hmm... I see your point. You think I can go over to Ali's and tell him I am sorry?" asked Ahmed.

"Sure, you can," said Dad with a smile. "But if you meet the bigger boys on your way, then..."

Before he could finish, Ahmed completed the sentence. "Then I will let them know they played super well today! I gotta go!" And with that, he hopped down the stairs and tumbled out the front door.

"Really—we need to have less noise in this house," said Mom with a laugh.

CHAPTER *Fifteen*

THE STORY OF PROPHET SULAYMAN (AS)

Prophet Sulayman (AS) was the son of Prophet Dawud (AS). He became king after the demise of his father and was well known for his compassion and justice.

Prophets are people chosen by Allah SWT to spread His message to others. Sometimes, they are also granted unusual gifts, such as the ability to perform miracles—allowing them to do things that other human beings are unable to do.

Prophet Sulayman (AS) was blessed with such a gift from Allah SWT. He could speak to the winds and tell them which directions to blow in. He could also understand the language of animals and speak to them—and they understood him as well. His army had humans and all kinds of animals, like birds and lions. He could even control the jinn and make them do his bidding. All of these were things that no other human could ever do. He also had knowledge of metallurgy, giving him the ability to make all kinds of weapons and other practical items.

Once, Prophet Sulayman's army was crossing through a valley while traveling. There was a colony of ants in the way. A little ant saw them and ran to tell the other ants: "O ants, enter your dwellings that you not be crushed by Sulayman and his soldiers while they perceive not."

Allah SWT enabled Prophet Sulayman (AS) to hear the little ant's conversation with her fellow ants. He smiled and thanked Allah SWT for His countless blessings and ordered his army to change its path so that they would not crush the colony of ants.

Sulayman (AS) had also built an enormous temple where people who believed in Allah SWT went to worship Him. They also went to Makkah for Hajj. One fine day, a hoopoe bird came to see Prophet Sulayman (AS). He told him that he had seen a place called Sheba, where the people were content with their lives and had everything they needed, but instead of thanking Allah SWT for their blessings, they worshiped the sun. The bird further added that this place was ruled by a queen.

Prophet Sulayman (AS) sent the bird back to the queen with a letter telling her about Allah SWT and inviting her to worship Him instead of the sun. The queen was confused and didn't know what to do, so she sent a gift back to Prophet Sulayman (AS) with her messengers, just so they could report back to her with information about him and his people.

When her messengers went to visit Prophet Sulayman (AS), they were amazed by the sight of his huge army, which included both humans and the animals under his dominion. They also saw the huge temple and a palace made of gold and were very awestruck. Prophet Sulayman (AS) told them he had no intention of taking their gift and only wanted them to worship Allah SWT. They went back and informed their queen about the incident. She then decided to visit Prophet Sulayman (AS) herself.

Before she arrived, Prophet Sulayman (AS) arranged to have the queen's throne brought forth in the blink of an eye.

The queen was amazed by this and the other things she saw, such as the ornate palace with its miraculous glass floors that is mentioned in the Quran. She understood that such miracles were from a higher power that was much greater than the sun she worshiped. In fact, such miracles could only emanate from Allah SWT, the Creator of the sun and of the entire universe.

In the end, this is how the queen and her people started believing in Allah SWT and stopped worshiping the sun.

CHAPTER
Sixteen

ASHAB AL-KAHF
(THE COMPANIONS OF THE CAVE)

It was more than a century after the demise of Isa (AS), and there were a few pious individuals living in the Roman Empire who believed in the Oneness of Allah against the wishes of the cruel emperors of their time. These cruel emperors wanted to kill the believers in order to set an example for others and prevent them from practicing their faith.

Wishing to escape persecution, a group of young believers fled with their dog one day to the mountains near their village and took refuge in a cave.

The youths were extremely frightened because the emperor's army was following them to capture them and get a bounty from the emperor. They prayed to Allah SWT with strong faith in their hearts to save them from the emperor's army. After their prayer to Allah SWT, they lay down to get some rest while their dog stood guard in front of the cave to protect the young believers against the tyranny of the army.

Allah SWT listened to their prayers and helped the pious youths. They all fell into a deep sleep along with their dog. Amazingly, they stayed asleep for three hundred years! During this time, they remained safe and sound, and no harm came to them or their dog.

When they woke up, however, they thought that they had been asleep for only a few hours. Glory be to Allah! Although they had been asleep for three hundred years, their bodies remained youthful, with no signs of aging or even a single sore or bruise. This was because Allah SWT had made them turn from side to side in their sleep so that no harm would come to their bodies.

They all felt hungry, so one of them went down to the village to get some food. There, he saw that it was not the same village as before. Of course, he did not realize that three hundred years had passed while he and his companions were asleep. But the thing that surprised him the most was that everyone in that village was practicing the true religion of belief in One God.

The young man went to a shop where he attempted to use his old coins from three hundred years ago to pay for the food. The shopkeeper was shocked to see the old coins and inquired about the young man's story, as the youth also seemed unfamiliar with his surroundings. The young man told the shopkeeper about himself and his friends in the cave.

Their story reached the king, who summoned the companions of the cave. The king listened to their story firsthand and was both amazed and inspired. He asked them to stay and live among the people.

It is important to note that these young believers were not messengers or prophets of Islam. They were just pious young men who stood firm in their belief in Allah SWT. In turn, the

Creator blessed them with His infinite mercy that kept them safe as they slept for three hundred years and then woke up to find a world in which they could freely worship Allah in an atmosphere of peace and safety. Allah SWT has mentioned this story in Surat al-Kahf (Chapter 18 of the Quran).

No matter what the hardship, Allah SWT is always there to help and protect us. We can make our faith in Allah SWT stronger by remembering to call out to Him whenever we are in need, whether it is a matter of huge importance, such as an exam, or something less critical, such as a broken shoelace! May Allah SWT guide and bless us all!

CHAPTER Seventeen

THE STORY OF PROPHET ISA (AS)

The story of Prophet Isa (AS) is extra special because his mother Maryam (AS) was extraordinary as well. Her parents Imran and Hannah had no children for a long time, so they used to pray regularly to Allah SWT for a child. Allah SWT listened to their prayers and granted their wish with a daughter. They named their daughter Maryam.

Maryam's mother had made a promise to Allah SWT that her unborn child would worship Him in the temple every day—and this is how Maryam (AS) spent most of her childhood. It was decided that Prophet Zakariyya (AS) would look after her, and he did. There was a special room for her in the temple that only he was allowed to enter.

One day, he went there and saw that there were all kinds of special fruits in her room that he hadn't brought for her. So, he asked her where they had come from, and she told him that Allah SWT had given them to her because the Creator "provides for whom He wills." Zakariyya (AS) realized that Maryam (AS) was a very special girl and took very good care of her.

At a certain point, we know from the Quran that Maryam (AS) "withdrew from her family to a place toward the east." While she was in seclusion, an angel visited her and told her that she would soon have a baby boy. She became very worried, because she did not even have a husband. But the angel told her that this was a special miracle from Allah, and that she should not worry.

Soon afterward, Maryam's baby was born. Maryam (AS) was very happy, but also worried about what people would say about her chastity. But then her baby Isa (AS) miraculously began to speak even though he was still only a newborn infant. He told Maryam (AS) that she shouldn't worry, and that he would tell the people the truth.

When she returned to her people, they started saying mean things about her. But then the baby began to speak. Naturally, the people were amazed by what they saw. They could not believe that a newborn baby could speak! Isa (AS) told them that he was a prophet with a book sent by Allah. Thus, they believed that the child was a miracle.

While he was growing up, Isa (AS) saw that the people weren't following the teachings of Prophet Musâ (AS), and this upset him greatly. He started telling people about Allah's message and the good deeds Allah SWT wants His people to do.

Isa (AS) was blessed by Allah and could do many extraordinary things. He had the ability to heal the sick and even give life to the dead by the permission of Allah SWT. Subhan Allah!

The disbelievers did not like Prophet Isa's miracles, and so they decided to kill him. They put him on a wooden cross and were about to kill him when Allah SWT protected him and took Prophet Isa (AS) back up to Heaven and replaced him with a similar looking man on the cross—and the evil people did not even notice.

CHAPTER Eighteen

RESPECT FOR THE ELDERLY

Omer had a little sister named Sakinah. It was summer vacation, and they were both very excited. This was going to be a special vacation. They were going to stay with their grandparents and their older cousin Rahim.

Mom was packing their bags and a few presents for Grandma, Grandpa, and Cousin Rahim. She called Omer and Sakinah and asked them to sit down. She was smiling, but her tone was serious. She said, "My dears, you know that Grandma and Grandpa are older than Mom and Dad, right?" Both Omer and Sakinah nodded. She continued, "They are your father's parents—and they are very special people. Make sure you are always kind to them and respect what they tell you to do."

The next morning, Omer and Sakinah hopped onto a bus and headed to their grandparents' house. The journey was long and tiring, but they had fun playing games and watching the many vehicles go by. At the bus stop, their cousin Rahim was waiting to pick them up. As soon as he saw them, he called out, "There you are—look at you two! The last time I saw you, you were just a little baby, Sakinah!" He picked up their luggage and headed to the car, where Grandpa was waiting for them, his face radiant with happiness.

Grandpa gave Omer and Sakinah a big hug and helped them fasten their seat belts for the short ride home. "Grandma has been cooking all day long," he told them as they turned into the driveway. The house was big with a great yard in which to play and catch frogs!

Grandma stood smiling at the front door. As soon as they entered the house, they could smell the delicious scents of the food wafting through the air, causing their tummies to growl! Rahim gave Grandma a quick hug and washed his hands before setting the table for dinner. He asked Grandma to sit down and then retrieved a pair of slippers for Grandpa and helped him ease into his chair.

They began to eat the delicious food—roasted chicken and potatoes followed by a yummy chocolate cake with strawberries on top! Grandma got up to clear the dishes, but Rahim stopped her. "Leave the cleaning to me. You must be exhausted after all of that cooking! Please relax while I put the kids to bed." Grandma's eyes shone with love. She patted Rahim on his back and kissed Omer and Sakinah goodnight before closing her bedroom door.

Rahim went to check on the children in the guestroom where their beds were. Omer asked, "Cousin Rahim, why do you live here?"

Rahim laughed and said, "Grandma and Grandpa are old now, and they need someone to take care of them. So, I found a job nearby, and I live here to help when I can! Now sleep tight, you two!" With that, he switched off the light and left.

"Did you see Cousin Rahim help Grandma and Grandpa?" Omer asked Sakinah. "He is so kind and helpful. I think this is what Mom meant when she said to be kind to Grandma and Grandpa."

"You're right," said Sakinah. "You know what? While we are here, let's help them out as well."

"Absolutely!" said Omer.

The next morning, the children woke up bright and early. Omer rushed downstairs to see what Grandpa was doing and helped him water the plants. Then he collected the mail from the mailbox and brought it inside. Meanwhile, Sakinah helped set the table and polish the glasses with a rag. She also helped Grandma cut fruit for breakfast. When Rahim came downstairs, he looked at the two hard at work and smiled. It made him happy to see his young cousins helping their elderly grandparents.

Grandma felt tired after the morning chores and sat down. Sakinah cuddled up next to her, and Grandma told her stories of her own adventures as a little girl. Sakinah loved the stories. She listened in respectful silence and laughed at the funny tales. Omer watched television with Grandpa while helping arrange his old books and other collectibles neatly in the large mahogany bookcase.

Throughout their vacation, the two children continued to help around the house. They never made noise while their grandparents were sleeping and always asked for permission before touching anything or going out to play. They watched Rahim and learned from his kind and gentle manners. They were delighted when they noticed Grandma and Grandpa making duaa for them each time one of them performed an act of kindness.

Sakinah said to Omer, "I am going to be the richest girl in town!"

Omer blinked at her and said, "What? You don't even have ten dollars to your name!"

Sakinah giggled. "You're so silly! But I do have loads and loads of duaas from Grandma and Grandpa!"

Omer laughed. "Me, too!"

CHAPTER
Nineteen

COOPERATION

Farhan stood shivering on the side of the road. He had been walking for about two hours now, and there was still no sign of any other living soul as far as the eye could see. His car had broken down, and his cell phone had lost its signal a while back. His legs were starting to ache, and the fear in the pit of his stomach was growing. "Am I going to freeze to death today?" he wondered. "O Allah, please don't let me die here. I'm so scared!"

He was just about to give up and sit down when he suddenly noticed a large object in the distance. His heart started beating faster as he squinted his eyes to make out what looked like a car parked several yards away. "O Allah! It definitely looks like a car! Please let someone be in it!" he prayed, his speed increasing along with the hope in his heart. He ran the last few steps and stopped when he reached the car.

He knocked on the window, but the young driver was busy on his phone and did not respond. Farhan tried again, and this time the driver heard him. He eyed Farhan warily as he slowly rolled the window down about an inch. "Who is it?" asked the driver, his voice trembling from the cold.

"As-salamu alaykum! My name is Farhan. My car broke down several hours ago, and I've been walking for a really long time.

I'm exhausted and freezing. Is it okay if I sit with you for a little while?"

There was silence followed by the click of car doors unlocking. Farhan ran to the other side and quickly got in. "Oh, al-hamdu-lillah!" said Farhan. Blessed relief from the cold!

"Wa-alaykum as-salam." The young man held out his hand. "I'm Sufyan."

"Nice to meet you, Sufyan! But why are you parked on the side of the road? Has your car broken down as well?" Farhan asked in despair.

"No, no, the car is fine. I just have very little gasoline left. I checked on my phone, and the station is only two miles away, so I can reach it, in sha' Allah." He paused and looked away.

"What's the matter, then?" Farhan asked curiously.

"I don't have money for fuel," Sufyan mumbled, his face flushed with embarrassment.

"Oh, that's not a problem at all!" Farhan said respectfully.

"How so?" asked Sufyan.

"We can help each other out! I can give you the money for the fuel, and you can help me reach my destination and get my car towed," Farhan explained.

"Are you sure?" Sufyan said hesitantly. "I don't want you to feel obligated to help me out. I would be happy to help you reach your destination regardless of the money."

"It's not a problem at all, my friend. You'd be the one helping me out. Besides, doesn't Islam teach us to help our brothers in need?"

Sufyan started the car and drove to the gas station. They filled the tank with gas and called for a towing service.

"Jazak Allah khayr for helping me in my time of need. I have found a great friend in my darkest moment!" said Farhan.

They agreed to stay in touch, and Sufyan waved his hand and smiled as he drove away.

CHAPTER
Twenty

LAYLAT AL-QADR
(THE NIGHT OF POWER)

It was almost the end of Ramadan, and it had been a joyful month at home. Khalid's mother, father, and elder sister Khawla had woken up together every morning for suhur and prayed all five prayers together every day as a family.

They had sat together reading the Quran, learning the teachings of Prophet Muhammad ﷺ, and spending time in dhikr and ibadah. It had been a wonderful month full of prayer and remembrance. On the first day of Ramadan, Khalid's father had promised him a great surprise on the twentieth night of Ramadan, especially if Khalid tried to fast for the entire month. Tonight was that very night, and Khalid had been fasting for several days. Since he was still learning, he would sometimes only fast half-days if he could not fast for the entire day.

"Baba, do you remember when you said that you would have a nice surprise for me on the twentieth night of Ramadan?" asked Khalid.

"Oh, yes! I do remember, and I am so glad that you remembered as well!" said his father.

"Can I see the surprise, please?" asked Khalid.

"The surprise is the greatest gift we get in the entire year," said his father. Then he called everyone to join him, and they sat down to listen to what he had to say.

"Do you know what Laylat al-Qadr is, Khawla?" asked the children's father.

"Yes, Baba," replied Khawla. "It is the Night of Power—the most special night of the entire year!"

"Yes! Let me tell you about this special night!" her father replied.

He began to recite Surat al-Qadr (Chapter 97 of the Quran), and then explained it to the children.

He said, "In this surah, Allah talks about Laylat al-Qadr. The Night of Power is the most valuable night of the best month in the year, because this was the night when Allah began to reveal the Quran to Prophet Muhammad, may the peace and blessings of Allah be upon him. The angel Jibril, alayhi al-salam, came to Prophet Muhammad, may the peace and blessings of Allah be upon him, and told him that this Night of Power would be greater than a thousand months, which is eighty-three years!"

Khalid said, "Wow! So, if I prayed on this night, it would be like I prayed for that long?"

"Yes! Absolutely!" replied his father.

Khalid asked, "But when is it? Which night is Laylat al-Qadr? I want to set an alarm so that I do not miss this great night!"

His father replied, "No one really knows when this night falls— but we do know that Prophet Muhammad, may the peace and blessings of Allah be upon him, guided us to look for this special night during the last ten nights of the holy month of Ramadan."

Khalid asked, "How can we look for it? Where can we find it?"

His father replied, "If you pray during these ten nights, give charity, or do any good deed, you will be lucky enough to find that night—and the rewards for all of your good deeds from that night will be multiplied many times over. This is a special blessing from Allah for all Muslims so that they will pray and ask for forgiveness and protection against the punishment of Hellfire."

"Shall I teach you a beautiful duaa that the Prophet's wife Aishah, may Allah be pleased with her, learned from Prophet Muhammad, may the peace and blessings of Allah be upon him, to recite on Laylat al-Qadr?" asked the children's father.

"Yes, please!" said Khalid and Khawla in unison.

"Allahumma innaka afuwwun tuhibbu al-afwa fa afu anni."
("O Allah, You are One Who forgives, and You love forgiveness, so forgive me.")

The whole family sat and learned this duaa together before their prayers that night so that they could find the Night of Power and be blessed with the mercy of Allah SWT.

CHAPTER
Twenty-One

PROPHET MUHAMMAD ﷺ
(PART ONE)

Prophet Muhammad ﷺ was the last prophet and messenger of Allah SWT.

Before him, prophets were sent for a specific time or for a specific nation—but Prophet Muhammad ﷺ was sent for everyone all over the world, until the end of time.

The Prophet's parents passed away when he was only a little boy. At the age of six, he went to live with his beloved grandfather Abd al-Muttalib, and then with his uncle Abu Talib at the age of eight. The young Muhammad ﷺ was a shepherd and took care of his uncle's sheep for him. He was loved and trusted by everyone due to his honest nature and kind personality, and was famously known as "the most honest" and "the most truthful" because of the great trust people had in his character.

Prophet Muhammad ﷺ grew up in Makkah and married Khadijah (RA), one of the most pious and wealthy women in Makkah. He had children with her as well.

The Prophet ﷺ was happy with his life, but seeing how the people of Makkah behaved greatly upset him. They were unkind to one another and built statues and idols that they worshiped as gods. The Prophet ﷺ would often seclude himself just to be alone with his thoughts and contemplate the reality of the world.

One day while the Prophet ﷺ was alone in a cave on Mount Hira, the angel Jibril (AS) came to see him and told him to read, but he did not know how to read. Jibril (AS) repeated his words another two times. Finally, he embraced Prophet Muhammad ﷺ tightly before the verses we now know as the first five verses of Surat al-Alaq (Chapter 96 of the Quran) were revealed.

The Prophet ﷺ went back to his wife, very scared and worried that he was imagining things. But she comforted him and told him that he was such a good person that Allah SWT would never bring harm to him. She took him to her cousin Waraqah ibn Nawfal, a pious man who had knowledge about the prophets. He told Prophet Muhammad ﷺ that he was a prophet of Allah, and that this experience was real!

After some time, the Prophet ﷺ was told by Divine revelation to start telling people about Allah SWT. So, he told his wife, and she accepted Islam, as did his cousin Ali (RA) and his best friend Abu Bakr (RA).

For many years, the Prophet ﷺ preached in secret because the disbelievers did not like the message of Allah SWT. Then when he started preaching openly and people began accepting Islam, the disbelievers got angry and began torturing the Muslims. Allah SWT gave the believers strength, and they never stopped believing in Allah SWT despite all of the torture they endured.

The disbelievers were very unkind to the Prophet ﷺ as well, but his uncle was there to protect him. After some time, Umar (RA), a very powerful individual within his tribe, also accepted Islam. This made the new Muslims stronger.

The disbelievers isolated the Muslims for three years and refused to let them exchange goods or food. They did not have a lot to eat and faced a very difficult time. Shortly afterward, the Prophet's wife and uncle, both of whom had been among his greatest supporters, passed away. He was very sad and missed them very much.

One night while Prophet Muhammad ﷺ was asleep, he went on a journey from Makkah to Jerusalem and then up to the heavens. He met other prophets, and Allah SWT gave him the special gift of five prayers a day so that the Muslims could ask Allah SWT for anything during their supplications. This important event was called the Isra and Miraj.

Some people came to meet Prophet Muhammad ﷺ from Yathrib, which is now known as Madinah. They accepted Islam and invited Prophet Muhammad ﷺ to go live there with them in peace and harmony.

Eventually, Prophet Muhammad ﷺ emigrated to Madinah with his Muslim followers in an event known as the Hijrah. The Muslims of Madinah (known as the Ansar) welcomed the Muslim emigrants from Makkah (known as the Muhajirun) with open hearts. The Ansar were very helpful and shared all of their belongings with the Muhajirun in a blessed atmosphere of faith and cooperation as they worked to build a strong Muslim community in Madinah.

CHAPTER
Twenty-Two

PROPHET MUHAMMAD ﷺ
(PART TWO)

I hope you remember yesterday's story about our beloved Prophet Muhammad ﷺ.

Do you remember where we left off?

Aaah yes, the Prophet ﷺ and his noble Companions (may Allah SWT be pleased with them all) had finally left for Madinah and were living in harmony with the Muslims there, who treated them with kindness and respect. They were finally happy. But it displeased the Prophet's tribe of Quraysh to see any happiness among the Muslims. This made them fight the Muslims from time to time.

Some battles were won by the Muslims, such as the Battle of Badr. Although they had very few men and horses to help them during this battle, they had great faith in Allah SWT. They lost other battles, however, even when they had lots of men and horses, such as what happened during the Battle of Uhud when they wrongly disobeyed the Prophet ﷺ.

One day, Prophet Muhammad ﷺ and his Companions decided to go for Umrah. But when they went to Makkah, the disbelievers would not grant the Muslim pilgrims entrance to the city. The Muslims, who came in peace and had no weapons with them, were able to successfully negotiate a peaceful agreement that allowed them to come back the following year for a period of three days. This truce between the two sides, which included other clauses and was supposed to last for a period of ten years, was known as the Treaty of Hudaybiyah.

Prophet Muhammad ﷺ sent letters and messengers to different faraway places, inviting the rulers of these lands to Islam. Some accepted Islam, and some did not.

It wasn't long, however, before the Quraysh, who were still up to their secret mischief, broke the peace treaty they had agreed to with the Muslims—so the Muslims decided to stop them once and for all. They marched to Makkah and peacefully took back the city. Prophet Muhammad ﷺ broke all of the statues and idols inside of the Kaabah and prayed there. When the disbelievers saw that the Muslims intended no harm to them, they embraced Islam in large numbers.

The Prophet ﷺ went back to Madinah as people continued to accept Islam. It was a happy time for the Muslims.

That same year, Prophet Muhammad returned to Makkah for what would be his final Hajj pilgrimage. Thousands of his Companions accompanied him on the journey, while many more came from other places. In his farewell sermon, he stood on Mount Arafat and told the people to be steadfast in their prayers and to be kind to each other—and the people also bore witness that Prophet Muhammad ﷺ had conveyed Allah's message to them and given them wise counsel throughout his prophethood. Now it was time for the people to pass along the message of Islam to others across the world.

Prophet Muhammad ﷺ went back to Madinah and became very ill there. He remained unwell for some time before he passed away in the home of his wife Aishah (RA). People were very sad about his demise, but Abu Bakr (RA) explained to them that the Prophet ﷺ was a human just like everyone else, and so he had indeed passed away, while only Allah SWT is eternal.

Prophet Muhammad ﷺ was buried in the same place in which he passed away. May Allah SWT bless him and help us follow his teachings and become good practicing Muslims.

CHAPTER
Twenty-Three

KINDNESS TO PEOPLE

In the early days, when Prophet Muhammad ﷺ had begun preaching the Oneness of Allah to the people of Makkah, the powerful nobles there became his enemies. They were very harsh toward the followers of Islam and the Prophet ﷺ alike. They badmouthed him and looked for every opportunity to hurt him, but our beloved Prophet Muhammad ﷺ never retaliated or said anything in response. He continued to preach the values of kindness, politeness, fairness, and respect. Not only did he preach these values, but he also believed in teaching through his actions.

Matters became a little better for the Muslims after the Prophet ﷺ and his faithful Companions (may Allah be pleased with them all) emigrated to Madinah and built an Islamic community there, but some people were still hostile toward Islam.

One day, when Prophet Muhammad ﷺ was walking on a road between Makkah and Madinah, he saw a group of young men who were yelling and mocking the sound of the adhan with meaningless words out of hatred for the Prophet ﷺ and the spread of Islam.

One of these young men in particular had a very distinctive and beautiful voice that caught the attention of the Prophet ﷺ. The young man's name was Abu Mahdhurah, and he was a resident of Makkah.

The Prophet ﷺ summoned Abu Mahdhurah in order to have a chat with him.

One can imagine how Abu Mahdhurah must have felt when he was singled out by the Prophet ﷺ, perhaps fearing that the Prophet ﷺ would be angry or even punish him for disrupting the call to prayer.

But Prophet Muhammad ﷺ was not angry; he instead smiled and gently caressed Abu Mahdhurah's forehead as he began teaching him the proper way to call the adhan. Abu Mahdhurah listened attentively as he repeated each phrase of the adhan after the Prophet ﷺ.

Abu Mahdhurah was deeply touched by the beautiful words he recited under the gentle guidance of the Prophet ﷺ and soon felt that the hatred in his heart had completely disappeared, instead becoming filled with light and love for the Prophet ﷺ and Islam.

After this, the Prophet ﷺ appointed Abu Mahdhurah to recite the adhan in Makkah, which he did for many years. Abu Mahdhurah was very happy to be honored in such a manner. He became known after that for never cutting his forelock, because the Prophet ﷺ had caressed it while teaching him the call to prayer.

As you may have heard before, actions speak louder than words, and this is why the Prophet's kind and gentle demeanor deeply affected Abu Mahdhurah (may Allah be pleased with him), showing him the truth and beauty of Islam. Simply saying something will never earn respect or friendship. But acting upon your good words inspires others to befriend you and believe in what you say.

Prophet Muhammad ﷺ was well known for good traits like kindness and honesty long before his prophethood was declared. In addition, his teachings about kindness, empathy, and love were for all of humankind, and not just the Muslims, because Allah SWT sent him with a message to the whole world for all times to come. He showed us that we must be kind in our behavior to both Muslims and non-Muslims. This is the only way that we can inspire others to follow in the footsteps of Muhammad ﷺ and emulate his beautiful teachings.

CHAPTER Twenty-Four

LOVING YOUR FAMILY

In the heart of a desert, there was a beautiful green oasis. The people of the oasis enjoyed the cool water, shade, and delicious fruit. The children who lived there were happy and chubby, and could often be seen rolling around in the sand under the cool shade of the palm trees. But one summer, there was a drought. The lake dried up, and water became difficult to find. The rich families still had plenty of food, while everyone else ate dates and scraps of dried meat.

Two brothers were among the residents of this oasis—Ahmed and Daud. Ahmed was a successful, rich merchant, while Daud was a shepherd. The drought caused many problems for Daud and his family. All of their sheep and cattle died due to the heat and lack of water.

One day, Ahmed came home from one of his trips. When he opened a box full of treats for the children, his oldest son Ali looked worried. Ahmed looked at Ali. "Son, is there something wrong?"

Ali replied, "Dad, when I saw Uncle Daud come home today, it looked like he didn't bring any food with him. Then I heard little Amina crying for a long time. I think she was hungry."

Ahmed looked at his boxes full of treats, food, and toys. He smiled at Ali and said, "Son, go get another box from the house so we can pack some things for little Amina. Put some sweets and fruit in there for her, too." Ali looked at the ripe fruit and suddenly felt confused. His own little brother, Saad, was enjoying a fistful of the delicious raisins. Ali did not want to take anything away from baby Saad.

Ali looked hesitantly at his father and said, "Can we leave the fruit for Saad? Look how much he likes it!"

Ahmed walked over to Ali and sat down on the ground next to him. "You love Saad, right?" Ali nodded. "Well, little Amina is your sister as well. She would love these raisins, too."

Ali said, "But, Dad, look at Saad! He has been eating the raisins since you opened the box! He seems to really love them a lot!"

Ahmed replied "Well, my son, then Amina will probably love them, too. More importantly, however, Allah will love you for doing such a kind deed for your family! Besides, look at Saad. He has eaten more than what is good for him, anyway."

Ali tweaked Saad's tiny little nose and packed up the fruit with the treats and toys. Ahmed and Ali walked over to Daud's house and knocked on the door. "Who is it?" Daud called out.

"Ahmed and Ali," Ahmed replied. Daud opened the door with a big smile as he invited them to come inside.

"Ali has brought little Amina some gifts!" said Ahmed.

When they walked inside, little Amina was sitting on the floor, sucking her thumb with her face swollen red from crying.

Ali rushed in and picked her up. He opened the box full of treats and fruit. He gave her a shiny new rattle and popped a raisin in her mouth. She giggled at the rattle and munched on the raisin, holding out her tiny hand for more. Amina's mother smiled.

As they walked home, Ahmed stroked Ali's head and said, "Son, always remember that you have a duty to your family and relatives. Whenever you have something to share, always share it with them. Be kind and thoughtful—just like you were today!"

Ali skipped the rest of the way home and said to Saad, "Tomorrow, you will share your new toys with little Amina. I will help you take them to her. We should be kind to our family because Allah loves us when we do. It makes us feel good inside, too!"

CHAPTER Twenty-Five

DON'T MAKE FUN OF PEOPLE

Dear children, do you know that making fun of people can be extremely hurtful? Sometimes what we may find funny can be a source of pain for others—and our Prophet Muhammad ﷺ warned against hurting other people. Let us read a story about two girls—one who found things funny even though it made the other girl sad.

Naimah had a younger sister named Amal. Amal was a toddler who was still learning how to walk as she went about stumbling and bumping into things all day long. Sometimes she would get hurt and yell out in pain, and sometimes she would get a bruise—and no one could be sure what had happened!

One day, Amal was running around as usual when she went into the kitchen. Naimah was working on her homework at the table. Amal ran past her and banged into the stove. A big pot of boiling water was on the flames and began to rock to-and-fro! As soon as Naimah saw what was happening, she leaped up from her chair and pulled Amal away from the stove. But some of the hot, boiling water splashed on Naimah's face. Naimah screamed, and her mother came running.

Naimah's parents took her to the hospital, where the doctors treated her for many days. Eventually, she began to feel much better. When Naimah looked in the mirror, however, she saw an angry red scar on her cheek and felt very bad. The kind doctor said that the scar would fade away in a few months. Naimah's parents were very upset about the accident, but they were also proud of Naimah for being brave enough to protect and save her little sister.

After a long summer vacation, it was now the first day of school, and Naimah was about to start fourth grade. Her pretty new dress was red with flowers on it and matched her shiny red bag.

Not only did she look absolutely wonderful and radiant, but she was also excited about the new term, her shiny new pencil case, and the many new things she would learn this year. When she walked onto the playground, however, she heard a loud snort followed by the sound of laughter.

"Ha, ha, ha, would you look at this girl!" cried out a tall burly girl sitting on the bleachers. "You sure have a funny face, Red Riding Hood!" The tall girl, whose name was Kulthum, pointed at Naimah and laughed, chanting out loud: Red face, red face! Pretty soon, a group of Kulthum's friends started chanting along with her. Naimah was very upset. She wanted to leave school and run home to her mother. But she took a deep breath and walked into her classroom instead.

During recess, the big girls were playing with the ball nearby while Naimah and her classmates sat eating their lunch. Suddenly, Naimah saw one of the girls falling, and before she even knew who it was, she jumped up to help break the fall, grazing her arm on some sharp pebbles in the process. The girl was Kulthum. Once again, Naimah had hurt herself while helping someone else.

Kulthum saw Naimah's arm bleeding and felt confused. She was embarrassed and thankful at the same time. She helped Naimah to the school nurse's office to get a bandage. In a kind voice this time, Kulthum asked Naimah, "Naimah, why do you have that scar on your face?" Naimah told her the story with tears in her eyes.

"You are one brave girl!" exclaimed Kulthum. "You saved baby Amal from getting seriously hurt, and today you saved me from bumping my head on the gravel. You are like a superhero!"

Naimah half-smiled and said, "You know, my scar will go away with time."

"Who cares! It's your battle scar—just like you see in the superhero comics!" said Kulthum. "Listen, I am truly sorry. I didn't know what happened, yet I made fun of you. That was very unkind of me. Can you forgive me?"

"Oh, that's okay. The important thing is that you don't think it's funny anymore! I would like to be friends, in sha' Allah," said Naimah.

"Why wouldn't I want to be friends with a superhero?" Kulthum asked as she helped Naimah back to class.

You see, making fun of people or laughing at them can be very unkind. We should always strive to be kind and thoughtful and never make fun of anyone. When we hurt someone, Allah SWT is displeased with us, and we must always strive to please Allah SWT by following in the kind and considerate footsteps of Prophet Muhammad ﷺ.

CHAPTER Twenty-Six

SAYING IN SHA' ALLAH

When Prophet Muhammad ﷺ declared his prophethood and began spreading the message of Islam, the people of Makkah did everything possible to oppose him.

They sent a group of men to some Jewish rabbis to ask them about Prophet Muhammad ﷺ, as they wanted to find out what their scriptures said about such a prophet. The men went to the Jews of Yathrib (the old name for Madinah), where the rabbis said that the people of Makkah should ask Muhammad ﷺ about three things, adding that only a true prophet of Allah would have knowledge of them.

They said, "First, ask him to tell you the story of some young men in the olden days. Then ask him to tell you the story of a man who traveled from one end of the world and reached the other end. Finally, ask him to tell you what the soul is. If he tells you about these things, then he is indeed a prophet, so follow his teachings and know that he is telling the truth. But if he does not know about these stories, then he is making it all up."

The men returned to Makkah and went to see Prophet Muhammad ﷺ in order to ask him these questions. Prophet Muhammad ﷺ replied that he would tell them what they wanted to know the next day—but he did not add "in sha' Allah" ("if Allah wills") to his statement.

The Messenger of Allah ﷺ never claimed anything before receiving a revelation from Allah SWT. So, he waited, but there was no revelation. Fifteen days went by, and still no revelation came. The men of Makkah were now beginning to get restless, and Prophet Muhammad ﷺ also became very sad.

Then, finally some verses of the Quran were revealed to Prophet Muhammad ﷺ containing all of the answers to the questions posed by the men of Makkah. In addition, a passage from Surat al-Kahf (Quran 18:23-24) also explained the proper manner in which Muslims should talk about future events:

"And never say of anything, 'Indeed, I will do that tomorrow,' Except [when adding], 'If Allah wills.' And remember your Lord when you forget..."

So, dear readers, whenever we make a decision or plan for the future, it is very important for us to always keep in mind the fact that everything that happens in life only happens according to Allah's will. We may plan for something and find that it does not turn out the way we want—and this could be because Allah SWT, in His infinite wisdom, knows that this plan is harmful for us at that particular time. It may also be that Allah SWT has a much better plan in store for us that we cannot even imagine. Understanding this allows us peace of mind as we surrender our will to what Allah SWT deems best for us.

In other words, the next time, you are planning something fun like a party or a soccer match, and you are excited because you think that your plan is the best plan ever, keep in mind that it is actually Allah SWT Who is the best of planners.

Even if your plans go ahead, don't go running out onto the soccer field yelling "We are going to win!" Instead, remember to add "in sha' Allah" ("if Allah wills"), and you will soon see the all of the blessings you are showered with, in sha' Allah. Likewise, when the party is about to start and you are excited about seeing your friends, remember to say, "We are going to have such a great time, in sha' Allah," and in sha' Allah you will!

CHAPTER Twenty-Seven

JUSTICE BETWEEN PEOPLE

The gray office complex was surrounded by a vast piece of land on which trees and bushes with wild berries growing on them could be found in abundance. Deer ran around freely in the many parks and pockets of wilderness. A few families of humble means lived just outside the office grounds and were employed by the office.

These families from the nearby village took care of the fruit trees and pruned the bushes. The men helped in the office to carry heavy loads in and out the buildings. Their children played all day long in the parks chasing butterflies and running around with each other.

Abdul-Rashid was the senior-most employee in the company, but he was new to this particular branch. He had recently moved to the area with his son and daughters. They came to see the grounds and were very happy to see all of the fruit trees and berry bushes. They planned to come back in summer to pick the ripened fruit and enjoy the yummy sweetness.

Abdul-Rashid was extremely knowledgeable about many things, but he was also a humble, quiet man with good manners. He treated his junior co-workers with great respect and was also very respectful to the men who helped carry the heavy loads.

With time, the other employees began to imitate his kind and respectful ways.

When summer finally came, the trees were loaded with fruit, and the berries shined in the bushes. Some of Abdul-Rashid's children came to spend a day at the grounds. Accompanied by a few helpers from the nearby village, they began to pick the fruit and gather the berries. It was a long day of hard work, but they gathered lots of delicious fruit! In the evening, Abdul-Rashid's eldest son stood commanding the men to load all of the fruit and berries into his father's car. With sadness in their eyes, the men quietly began to load the fruit. They were very poor and could not afford to buy the same type of delicious fruit for their families. The men's little children saw this and were very disappointed because they had hoped that they would also get to enjoy the fruit.

Abdul-Rashid came out of the building to go home, but stopped when he noticed that the usually happy children were huddled together under a barren tree. He felt uneasy at this sight and wondered why they looked so sad. Then when he reached his car, he saw box upon box of sweet-smelling ripe fruit loaded into the trunk.

Abdul-Rashid turned to his son and said, "Son, did you give the children from the village their share?"

Saqib blushed and said, "No, Baba, we are in charge of the land now, and this is our fruit! Plus, Naimah and Amna are also waiting for the fruit back at home!"

Abdul-Rashid placed a loving hand on his son's shoulder and said,

"These workers live on these lands. This land belongs to Allah SWT before anyone else, so who are we to say that we will not share? Our Prophet Muhammad, may the peace and blessings of Allah be upon him, has taught us to be fair and ensure justice! So, it is fair that the people who actually live on the land and help pick the fruit get their share, right?"

Saqib nodded his head and began unloading the car as he counted out boxes to divide equally among the men. Abdul-Rashid went to his son again and said, "I am proud of you because you learn so fast, but listen to me, son. Al-hamdu lillah, the truth is that we are very well-off and can afford to buy any kind of fruit we like whenever we feel like it, isn't that right?"

Saqib said, "Yes, Baba! We do that every week!"

"Exactly," his father said with a smile. "So, it is only just that we give the workers a larger share of this fruit while we only take a small share home to taste. The workers cannot afford to buy this type of fruit, but our situation is different, and we should be mindful of that."

Saqib stood looking at the little children and their sad faces. "Baba, thank you for helping me see the difference between equality and justice. I have learned something very important today!"

After this, Saqib left just two boxes for his family and with a big smile gave the rest of the fruit to the workers and their children. He even played tag with the children for a while before returning to his father.

"Baba, this fruit will taste so much sweeter because of the great lesson I learned today!" said Saqib on the way home.

Abdul-Rashid said, "Al-hamdu lillah, you have made me very proud. I pray you will remember to keep this lesson in mind whenever you deal with people in the future as well."

CHAPTER Twenty-Eight

LEARN TO SHARE

The greatest example of sharing in the history of humankind took place when the Muslims of Makkah emigrated to Yathrib, an older name for the blessed city of Madinah.

The Muslims of Makkah left their beloved city during a difficult period. The disbelievers of Makkah had been treating the Muslims harshly and making it very difficult for them to practice Islam. With the blessings of Prophet Muhammad ﷺ, small groups of Muslims began to leave Makkah for Madinah.

On the other side of the desert, the Muslims of Madinah (known as the Ansar) were prepared to welcome their brothers and sisters in faith with generosity and kindness. When the Muslim emigrants from Makkah (known as the Muhajirun) reached Madinah, they had nothing. They had left everything behind and were now in a strange land. The Ansar of Madinah welcomed them with open doors and open arms!

Prophet Muhammad ﷺ paired every Muslim from Makkah with a Muslim from Madinah as brothers or sisters. The Ansar set the greatest example of sharing. They shared their food, homes, and properties with their emigrant brothers and sisters. Some even gave half of their businesses to the Muhajirun.

One of the Prophet's Companions from Madinah took his brother from Makkah to his home and said to his wife, "Generously serve this guest of Prophet Muhammad, may the peace and blessings of Allah be upon him." His wife replied that there was only enough food for the children. The great Companion of the Prophet ﷺ asked her to share the food with the emigrant brother. They went hungry that night but made sure that their guest ate well and slept peacefully. Allah SWT has decreed a great reward for this noble deed in the Hereafter, in sha' Allah.

So, my dear readers, learn to share and be generous with your charity. There are many ways in which a person can share with others!

In school, for example, you can help your friends learn by sharing your knowledge with them. Tutoring a friend when he or she has been absent due to illness is a form of sharing.

When you know that there are people in need who can benefit from your help, offer it to them. Volunteer for causes that help the poor, the needy, the elderly, and the disabled. The time you give to such causes will bring joy to the people you are helping, and you will also be rewarded for your good deeds by Allah SWT, in sha' Allah.

Charity is the best way to share your worldly belongings with people who are less fortunate. Share your toys with children who might not have as many as you do. Give away your books and clothes while they are still in good, usable condition.

The more your share, the more thawab (rewards from Allah SWT) you will collect, in sha' Allah.

A small act of kindness and generosity can also help you make friends and as you work hard to build a strong and caring community together—just like the Ansar who helped the Muhajirun when they first arrived in Madinah, establishing the foundations for a strong Muslim ummah (nation).

Let us learn from these great deeds and do our part to make our own communities strong and happy for everyone.

CHAPTER Twenty-Nine

BEING NEIGHBORLY

Islam is a religion that places great emphasis on kindness and humility. The way people care for one another is one of the most beautiful aspects of a Muslim community. Let's read the story of how our beloved Prophet Muhammad ﷺ exhibited kindness to his neighbors regardless of things like age, religion, or social status.

One day, Prophet Muhammad ﷺ learned that a Jewish neighbor, who was a servant boy of his in Madinah, had fallen ill, so the Prophet ﷺ went to visit him in his home. The fact that the boy and his family practiced a different religion did not deter the Prophet ﷺ from showing concern for the boy, nor did it matter to him that the boy was young or worked as a servant.

The Prophet ﷺ showed great compassion to the boy during his visit, even sitting near the spot where the boy's head was resting.

One can imagine how the boy felt during this visit, as it would have been a great honor for the respected Prophet of Islam to make a special trip just to see him and make sure that he was okay. As seen in many other authentic stories about the life of Prophet Muhammad ﷺ, it was part of the Prophet's exemplary character to always show humanity in such situations.

Such stories also show us that Prophet Muhammad ﷺ used to like children, boys and girls alike, and that they used to like him, too! This is because he was always kind to them, showing respect for them and listening attentively to their concerns. He did not ever feel bored of their talk and would even play with them and carry them on his back.

The Jewish boy described above embraced Islam during the Prophet's visit, and his father, who was also there, encouraged him to do so although he himself was also Jewish.

What we learn from the Prophet's example is that we owe it to our neighbors to be kind and caring. It is our duty to be concerned about their well-being, and to care for them in their times of need. Another lesson we learn is that our own kindness can influence other people. The boy and his father were impressed by Prophet Muhammad ﷺ, and it was his unexpected kindness that convinced the boy to embrace Islam with the permission and encouragement of his father.

Prophet Muhammad ﷺ has shown us through countless examples how to be thoughtful of our neighbors' needs. An important teaching of his says that: "He who eats his fill whilst his neighbor beside him goes hungry is not a believer."

The great benefit of being kind to neighbors is that it helps us build strong communities in which we take care of each other. Today, an elderly neighbor may need a ride to the doctor or grocery store, while tomorrow it may be you who needs help with something else. Being kind to neighbors increases our thawab (rewards from Allah SWT) and helps our neighborhoods become more pleasant to live in as well.

CHAPTER Thirty

THE BLESSED EID

Today was the twenty-ninth day of Ramadan. Everyone in the house was waiting for the iftar meal that would break their fasts when Maryam suddenly wailed out to her mother with tears ready to spill out of her eyes, "Will Baba be here tonight like you promised?"

Her mother stroked her damp cheek and said softly, "It depends on the moon, sweetheart! Come help me pack the food that we will send to Baba." Maryam's father was observing itikaf in the masjid.

Maryam tried to conceal her disappointment. It had been nine long days since she had last seen her father. Even now, she was not sure when he would come back. The whole time, Mummy had been sending Baba food for both the suhur and the iftar.

"Why, Mummy?" asked Maryam angrily. "Why isn't Baba coming home, and what does the moon have to do with it? I miss him!"

Her mother hugged her tightly and said, "Baba is in the masjid observing itikaf. He will be there for nine or ten nights in the mosque, praying to Allah. It is a special time during which he is making duaa for all of us. Does that make sense?"

They sat down together and broke their fast with dates and sandwiches. When they were finished, Maryam's big brother Asad raced outside to see if he could spot the new moon.

Suddenly, there was clatter, a lot of running, and some stumbling before Asad ran back inside the house, yelling, "MUMMY! I SAW THE MOON!" Asad picked up Maryam and swung her around and around.

"Oh, that is lovely," said Mummy. "Al-hamdu lillah, that means that Baba will soon be home!"

Sure enough, in another hour or so, the door creaked open, and Maryam let out a shrill screech. "Baba!" The children's father rushed in and hugged everyone as he wished them a blessed Eid. Once everyone had dinner and settled down, the children wanted to know what itikaf had been like.

"It was the most beautiful ten days, my dears. I sat in the mosque with our Muslim brothers in faith all day long, praying and remembering Allah SWT. We thought about our shortcomings and asked Allah to help us become better Muslims. We also made duaa for Allah's blessings."

Mummy came in carrying a tray with two glasses of warm milk, "All right, children, let's get to sleep now. We have to be up bright and early for the Eid prayer tomorrow!"

The next morning, Baba, Mummy, Asad, and Maryam dressed up in their new Eid clothes and went to offer the Eid prayer at the mosque, where they listened to the imam as he told them about the significance of the Eid and the blessings of Ramadan.

He asked everyone to continue performing good deeds even though the holy month of Ramadan was now over.

When they came back home, Mummy gave them some of the delicious sweet treats she had made the night before. Soon, their friends and neighbors came over to wish everyone a blessed Eid.

Finally, after the *Asr* prayer, Baba took Asad and Maryam to a nearby hospital, where they distributed Eid presents to the sick children.

"Baba, why are we giving gifts to the sick children?" asked Maryam, feeling a little sad to see so many children in the hospital.

"My dear, the Eid is a special day full of joy. We have so many blessings from Allah, so we must thank Him by giving to others as well!"

On their way back home, Maryam saw a little girl who had fallen off her new bike. "Baba, stop!" yelled Maryam. She rushed out and helped the little girl up and said, "Oh, poor baby, don't cry. Here, take my bracelet. It is pretty and will help make you feel better!" The little girl looked at the pretty bracelet and giggled as she hugged Maryam and ran to her mother.

"Baba, I feel so happy in my tummy!" said Maryam, and everyone started laughing at Maryam's funny remark.

CONCLUSION

We pray that you and the precious children in your life enjoyed the stories in this book and benefited from the many priceless lessons of morality and kindness contained within each story. Allah willing, the stories have provided a foundation for more discussion and helped create a culture of Islamic learning at home (and school) throughout the blessed month of Ramadan.

Our hope is that these stories will help introduce children to important lessons that are vital for all young Muslims growing up in various societies around the world. To that end, keep revisiting these stories to track comprehension and learning progress as you continue to read the stories year-round.

Keeping the spirit of Ramadan alive long after the month has passed is one of the key reasons why we increase our acts of worship and other good deeds during the thirty days. As such, we pray that this book has provided a marvelous opportunity for all readers, young and old alike, to bond with Islamic teachings and adopt them as a way of life.

Please consider sharing this book with others who may benefit. A book of stories makes an excellent gift for the Eid and is also an appropriate gift for new parents who may be building up a library of educational books for their Muslim children. Your online reviews and social media posts recommending the book are also appreciated and will help spread the word.

May Allah SWT bless you and your families with a wonderful year ahead, until we meet again next Ramadan, in sha' Allah!

Printed in Great Britain
by Amazon